What Happens Next?
DEALING WITH LIFE CHANGES

What Happens When
I Have Hearing or Vision Loss?

Emiliya King

PowerKiDS press

Published in 2026 by The Rosen Publishing Group, Inc.
2544 Clinton Street, Buffalo, NY 14224

Copyright © 2026 by The Rosen Publishing Group, Inc.

First Edition

All rights reserved. No part of this book may be reproduced in any form without permission in writing from the publisher, except by a reviewer.

Editor: Caitie McAneney
Book Design: Leslie Taylor

Photo Credits: Cover Peakstock/Shutterstock.com; p. 5 wavebreakmedia/Shutterstock.com; p. 7 ANURAK PONGPATIMET/Shutterstock.com, (inset) snapgalleria/Shutterstock.com; p. 9 Nina Lishchuk/Shutterstock.com; p. 11 Steve Shoup/Shutterstock.com, (inset) Ivan_Shenets/Shutterstock.com; p. 13 hedgehog94/Shutterstock.com; p. 15 Wallenrock/Shutterstock.com, (inset) Yavdat/Shutterstock.com; p. 17 wavebreakmedia/Shutterstock.com, (inset) Zifalaniasta/Shutterstock.com; p. 19 fizkes/Shutterstock.com; p. 21 maxim ibragimov/Shutterstock.com.

Cataloging-in-Publication Data
Names: King, Emiliya.
Title: What happens when I have hearing or vision loss? / Emiliya King.
Description: Buffalo, NY : PowerKids Press, 2026. | Series: What happens next? dealing with life changes| Includes glossary and index.
Identifiers: ISBN 9781499452600 (pbk.) | ISBN 9781499452617 (library bound) | ISBN 9781499452624 (ebook)
Subjects: LCSH: Children with disabilities–Juvenile literature. | Hearing disorders in children–Juvenile literature. | Vision disorders in children–Juvenile literature
Classification: LCC HQ773.6 K46 2026 | DDC 362.4083–dc23

Manufactured in the United States of America

Some of the images in this book illustrate individuals who are models. The depictions do not imply actual situations or events.

CPSIA Compliance Information: Batch #CSPK26. For Further Information contact Rosen Publishing at 1-800-237-9932.

CONTENTS

The Five Senses 4

Trouble with Hearing. 6

Hearing Tests. 8

Supports for Hearing Loss. 10

Struggling to See. 12

Testing Your Vision 14

Helpful Skills and Support. 16

Communicating with Others 18

You Can Do Anything! 20

Glossary. 22

For More Information 23

Index 24

The Five Senses

How do you take in **information** about the world around you? Think about the things you may see, hear, taste, smell, and touch. Those are your five senses, and they help you **experience** the world.

Your senses tell your brain what's around you. This keeps you safe. For example, you see a car coming, so you don't walk across the street. You hear thunder, so you come inside. However, some people have trouble hearing or seeing things like others do.

Your Point of View

People who have trouble hearing as they should may identify themselves as deaf or hard of hearing.

People who have trouble seeing as they should may identify themselves as blind or visually **impaired**.

5

Trouble with Hearing

Ears take in sound waves, which **vibrate** little parts in the inner ear. Sound waves turn into electrical signals that go to the brain.

Some people are born without the ability to hear. Others are hard of hearing, or struggle to hear things that aren't very loud. It can be caused by problems with the ears at birth, infections, or being around very loud sounds. Some hearing loss is because of problems with the inner ear. Other kinds have to do with the connection between the inner ear and brain.

If you have hearing loss, you may have trouble hearing people speak. That can make school and **socializing** a challenge without the right supports.

Cochlea

Your Point of View

Some hearing loss has to do with a snail-shaped part of the inner ear called the cochlea.

Hearing Tests

Babies are checked for hearing when they're born. If you're born with hearing loss, you may have already learned to live your life without this sense. However, if you lose your hearing later on, you may not know what's wrong or what to do next.

You can go to your doctor. They may send you to an audiologist, which is a **specialist** who can test people for hearing loss. They will see which sounds you can hear, from high pitches to low ones.

Your Point of View

If you have ear infections often, you may have a hard time hearing from time to time. Doctors will test your hearing at checkups.

Once you are **diagnosed** with hearing loss, you can get the help you need to experience the world.

9

Supports for Hearing Loss

If you have hearing loss, there are people and things that can help you. Some hearing loss from ear infections, ear wax buildup, and injury to the ear can be fixed through medicine, wax removal, or operations. People may also use hearing aids or other listening devices.

People with lifelong hearing loss often learn sign language. Letters and words are shown with hand shape and motion. Some people learn to read lips to know what people are saying. They may read text called "closed captioning" on the TV.

Some people with hearing loss use a service animal to help them get around and alert them to sounds.

cochlear implant

Your Point of View

People who have issues with the cochlea, in the inner ear, may get a cochlear implant to help them take in sounds.

Struggling to See

Just like the ears, eyes are meant to take in information and send it to the brain. Parts in your eyes work together to sense light and pictures. Special nerves send that to the brain so the brain can figure out what it is.

Many people have blurry eyesight, which can be fixed with glasses or contacts. Other people see only shadows or very blurry shapes. Other people can't see anything at all out of one or both eyes.

Your Point of View

While blindness can be caused by injury or illness, it can also be present at birth.

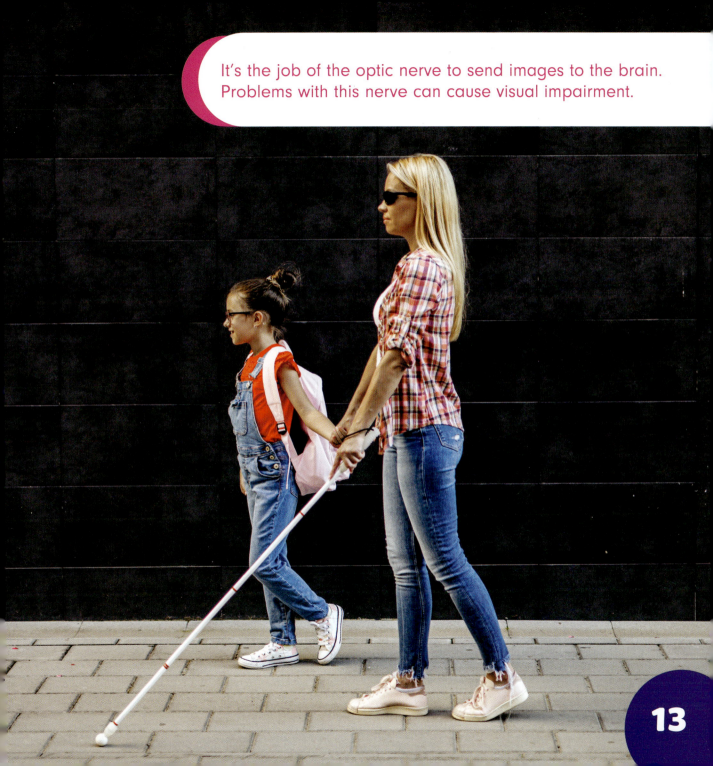

It's the job of the optic nerve to send images to the brain. Problems with this nerve can cause visual impairment.

Testing Your Vision

As with hearing, doctors usually test a baby for vision early on. As you get older, you'll look at an eye chart with letters of different sizes to see what you can see. Tell your doctor if you're having trouble with vision.

Doctors can check to see if your vision problems are due to cataracts, or clouded lenses in the eye. They can tell if eyes are "crossed," or looking at different angles. Without correction, this can lead to a "lazy eye," or poor vision in one eye.

Your Point of View

If you have family members with vision loss, you are more likely to have it. It can be genetic.

Your doctor may test your eyes at your yearly checkup.

Helpful Skills and Tools

Glasses and contacts can help with many cases of blurry vision. Operations to fix the eyes can help too. However, if a person is considered blind, they can get extra support to live with the condition.

Some people with blindness learn how to read braille. Things written in braille have letters spelled out with raised bumps so they can be read by touch. Some people use canes to find any **obstacles** in their way. Some have service animals to guide them.

Braille helps people with blindness learn to read.

Your Point of View

People with blindness can use screen readers, which read aloud any content that is shown on a computer or TV screen.

17

Communicating with Others

When people talk to one another, it is usually through spoken words. When people do **gestures** or show their feelings on their face, it's something that must be seen to be understood. This can make it hard for people with hearing and vision loss to communicate as others do.

If you are going through this, remember that you can do hard things. You may need to communicate differently, but it is possible to learn, chat, and **express** yourself. Programs can teach you how to speak sign language or read braille, for example.

Let others know what you need to be able to understand something. For example, if you are hard of hearing, you can tell people to speak up.

Your Point of View

It can help to talk to others who are going through the same things as you. Groups for people with hearing and vision loss can make you not feel so alone.

You Can Do Anything!

Kids with vision and hearing loss can do anything that their peers can do. They can play sports, make art, play instruments, and learn in school. Famous musician Ray Charles (1930–2004) was blind yet expressed himself through music. Superbowl champion Derrick Coleman is legally deaf yet made a career in pro football.

Ask for support when you need it. Devices like hearing aids and glasses can help. Service animals, canes, and screen readers can too. Your teachers and therapists can give you the knowledge you need to overcome your challenges.

People who are blind often have an incredible sense of hearing. Focus on what you *can* do, not what you can't.

Your Point of View

Helen Keller (1880–1968) was a famous author and teacher who was both blind and deaf yet traveled the world speaking up for **disability** rights.

Glossary

diagnose: To identify a disease by its signs and symptoms.

disability: A condition that impairs or limits a person's ability to do certain tasks or participate in daily activities.

experience: To do something or to take it in through the senses.

express: To communicate what you're thinking or feeling.

gesture: A movement usually of the body or limbs that shows an idea or feeling.

impaired: Lacking full function or ability.

information: Knowledge or facts about something.

obstacle: Something that stops forward movement or progress.

socialize: To participate in a social group or spend time with others.

specialist: A person who studies or works at a special occupation.

vibrate: To make small movements.

For More Information

Books

Knight, A. J. *Hearing Loss*. Vancouver, BC: Engage Books, 2023.

Leavitt, Hannalora, and Sarah Harvey. *Vision Loss*. Vancouver, BC: Engage Books, 2023.

Websites

Blindness
kidshealth.org/en/kids/visual-impaired.html
Learn more about living with blindness.

What's Hearing Loss?
kidshealth.org/en/kids/visual-impaired.html
Explore the different kinds of hearing loss and how they're treated.

Publisher's note to educators and parents: Our editors have carefully reviewed these websites to ensure that they are suitable for students. Many websites change frequently, however, and we cannot guarantee that a site's future contents will continue to meet our high standards of quality and educational value. Be advised that students should be closely supervised whenever they access the internet.

Index

A

audiologist, 8

B

braille, 16, 17, 18
brain, 4, 6, 12, 14

C

Charles, Ray, 20
cochlear implant, 11
Coleman, Derrick, 20

D

disability rights, 21
doctors, 8, 14, 15

E

ear infections, 8, 10

G

gestures, 18
glasses, 12, 16, 20

H

hard of hearing, 4, 6, 19
hearing aids, 10, 20

K

Keller, Helen, 21

O

operations, 10, 16

S

senses, 4, 8, 12, 21
service animals, 11, 16, 20
sign language, 10, 18